Am I pig enough for you yet?

Also by Valerie Shaff and Roy Blount Jr.

If you only knew how much I smell you:
  True portraits of dogs

I am puppy, hear me yap:
  The ages of dog

Am I pig enough for you yet?

Voices of the barnyard

Photographs by Valerie Shaff

Text by Roy Blount Jr.

HarperCollins*Publishers*

For her who lives near the forest of pigs—R. B.

To not crying over spilled milk—V. S.

AM I PIG ENOUGH FOR YOU YET? Photographs copyright © 2001 by Valerie Shaff
and text copyright © 2001 by Roy Blount Jr. All rights reserved. Printed in Japan.
No part of this book may be used or reproduced in any manner whatsoever
without written permission except in the case of brief quotations embodied in
critical articles and reviews. For information, address HarperCollins Publishers Inc.,
10 East 53rd Street, New York, NY 10022.

HarperCollins books may be purchased for educational, business, or sales
promotional use. For information, please write: Special Markets Department,
HarperCollins Publishers Inc., 10 East 53rd Street, New York, NY 10022.

FIRST EDITION

Printed on acid-free paper

Library of Congress Cataloging-in-Publication Data
Shaff, Valerie.
Am I pig enough for you yet? : voices of the barnyard / photographs
by Valerie Shaff; text by Roy Blount Jr.—1st ed.
p.   cm.
ISBN 0-06-019487-1
1. Photography, Humorous. 2. Domestic animals—Humor—Pictorial
works. 3. Photography of livestock. I. Blount, Roy. II. Title.
TR679.5 .S53 2001
779'.32—dc21   2001024075

01 02 03 04 05 ❖/TOP 10 9 8 7 6 5 4 3 2 1

Acknowledgments

There are a number of people whose contributions have brought this book to fruition—many of whom have begun to feel a bit like family, as this has been our second endeavor together and the making of a book is a prolonged birth. Thanks to my agent and friend Janis Donnaud, and my editors Larry Ashmead and Krista Stroever. Since my contribution to this book is visual, I'm particularly grateful to those who make the transition from my photographic prints to a printed page as smooth as possible. For this great labor I thank Lucy Albanese, Roni Axelrod, John Hanley, Sarah Gubkin, and Cindy Achar. Thanks also to Katharine Pollak, who hand develops all of my film and is always there for me quietly running her one-woman show.

These farm animal photographs were of course inspired by the beauty and fascination of the subjects, but I have found animals to be available to commune with me in direct proportion to how they are treated by the people in their lives. It's only natural. Many thanks to all of the men and women who happily agreed when I asked if I might join their animals in the field or barn to photograph them.

Special thanks and much admiration go to a few individuals who have found wonderful ways to enhance the lives of both the animals and the people whom they have made it their business to bring together: Paul Kupchok of Green Chimneys; David Meeks; Vincent and Linda Scaturro; Lenny Miller; Susie Reichelt; Barbara Sweeney of the Southlands Foundation; and Ellen Pearson. Lastly, I'd like to thank John Hull, whose timeless third generation farm first inspired this work.

—Valerie Shaff

Thanks to Janis, the best animal-packager since Noah.

—Roy Blount Jr.

Introduction

BY ROY BLOUNT JR.

Cows, for instance. You know how the song goes: you shouldn't try to understand them, just rope and tie and brand them. But I can't help wondering. What would it be like to be one? I'd be too anxious.

> I stand out here from dawn to dusk a-ruminating, yet
> I haven't thought of anything illuminating yet.

I doubt I could console myself with what cows probably do fall back on:

> The reason why, I think, is that instead of gains and losses,
> What I'm into, bottom line, is . . . whatchamacallit. Process.

On the other hand, I'm not fidgety enough to be a chicken, at least in the daytime.

> Chickens in the bread pan, pecking up dough.
> Mama, can't we take a break? No, child, no.

Pigs, I know, are smart and also down to earth, a combination I applaud. But if I were one, I'm not sure I would be as comfortable in my skin as pigs seem to be.

> The other day
> They leaned on my fence
> And said, "They say
> Pigs are smart."
>
> Well, there's a sense
> In which people are fat.
> We must not lay
> Too much on that.
>
> "Whatta *you* say?"
> They then asked me.
> I let a big fart
> And let them be.

To look at Valerie Shaff's photographs is to be reminded of how well pigs handle being pigs, cows cows, chickens chickens. So who are we to have identity crises?

Before Valerie ever became dog photographer to the rich and famous, it was cows and chickens and pigs that drew her out of a depression. "I was in a bad state of mind," she says, "until I started hanging out with farm animals. I love barns and the smell of barns, and there's nothing like climbing over a split-rail fence and getting in with the animals. They're so funny. You can't manipulate them—it's more like . . . well, it's not exactly like sports photography because it's not that fast, but it's waiting and watching.

"If they've been somewhat mistreated, they're a bit skittish. But if you go to a small farm like the ones where these pictures were taken—these farmers are practical; they're not anthropomorphic like I am, but they treat the animals with humanity, and the animals respond. I'll be getting goosed by one pig while trying to photograph another one. They get *too* close, stick their face right into the camera. I have to back off because I've got a wet nose inside my lens."

I have never worked that closely with pigs myself, but I have had some experience in animal husbandry, and . . . If I sound a bit defensive on this score, it is because of one isolated relationship with a rooster.

I have never had a barn, but for quite a while during the Reagan administration I did help give a home, in and around my garage, to an old horse named Ollie and three free-range chickens: two hens, Flo and Lois, and a rooster, Jack. When the chickens circulated together, Jack generally appeared to be in the lead—an impression he managed to convey by figuring out where the hens were headed and then scooting, in an odd hoisting-of-the-skirts posture that suggested a scrambling archbishop, around in front of them. At least that's the way it looked to me. Once situated, he would draw up all stately, extend one foot forward ver-r-r-ry slowly while darting his head about in surveillance (mostly, I think, for the effect of the comb-toss) and going "buuuuuuuuuk" in a low voice implying an as-if-effortless-yet-by-no-means-facile assumption of the awful burden of command—and then, when the leading foot finally touched the ground, there was a moment when Jack appeared to have frozen into a monument to poultry masculinity. And *then* he would shift his weight dramatically forward, hold that stance for a beat, and begin the process again. Walk of the cock. The hens meanwhile would be muttering and scratching up sustenance. Sometimes when they drifted away from Jack's train he would turn, go "brerrk?," gather up his lower plumage, take a running jump, and briefly, inappropriately, mount one or the other of them. Their response was always to squawk, ruffle up, shake, and get back to pecking in the dirt.

By way of apology for my gender, and also just experimentally, I would scatter a variety of tidbits. Cheese doodles the chickens pecked at and tossed aside, but when I dumped in front of them a pile of croutons that had gone stale, croutons and chickens dissolved into a blur of dust, crouton crumbs, and feathers. When the air cleared, there were no croutons, just chickens, blinking and catching their breath. I think this is about as much as you will ever get out of chickens in the way of gratitude. I wrote a little jingle, in French:

> *Les poulets sont dans les croûtons—*
> *Mais . . .*
> *Oú sont les tous les deux maintenant?*
> *C'est . . .*
> *Merveilleux, n'est-ce pas? Voyez:*
> *Les croûtons sont dans les poulets.*

At first Jack had tolerated my presence around the place, but maybe he felt I crossed some line with his hens, or he may just have resented, as I might in his place, being treated as a figure of whimsy. After he caught me doing an imitation of his walk for visitors, he began to lurk behind things and leap out at me like Inspector Clouseau's Asian valet. In fact he would make, deep in his throat, nearly the same karate noises. When I stepped out the back door he would fly up almost as high as my face, brandishing his spurs at me. Not wanting to yield alpha-male status to a chicken, I kept a stick by the door to brandish at him. Sometimes I was in the mood for this, but not always. Once or twice I had to whap him with the stick—not a pleasant sensation, in part because it so clearly confirmed his opinion of me. Eventually he would sidle off a bit, muttering, "Let that be a lesson to you"—always at pains to maneuver in such a way that no one could accuse him of anything worse than accepting a standoff. A couple of times he got in a good lick of his own. You hate to tell people you're late arriving somewhere because you had to whack your rooster with a stick and then go back in the house and put antiseptic on the scratch he left on your arm and then come back out and fend him off again.

The hens earned their keep by laying eggs—sometimes clandestinely here and there in the garage, where the eggs would go very bad, but usually in their nests, where we could harvest them; and since Flo and Lois enjoyed a rich diet of bugs and scraps as well as standard feed, their eggs had character even when fresh. Aside from crowing at unpredictable hours, Jack didn't contribute anything so far as I could see. Perhaps because he put so much of his energy into status preservation and challenging me, none of the hidden eggs produced chicks, and I felt that our dogs, who took a wary, familial interest in Flo and Lois that Jack affected to ignore, could protect the hens against predators. So I placed a candid classified ad in *The Shopper's Guide*: "Free. One aggressive rooster. Come get him someone please."

A soft-spoken lady showed up. Was I sure this rooster was good and aggressive, she asked. That was the kind of rooster she needed, to guard her flock. Don't worry about that, I said. I stepped out in front of Jack and braced myself. He took one look at me and fled as if terrified. I ran after him. He hightailed it into the woods. I thrashed about, diving at him. He zigzagged, squawking in unwonted tones of innocent astonishment. I tried several times to throw a blanket over him. He dodged it every time. I lost my hat and glasses. He ran around pleading for an explanation. Finally my son brought him down with a flying tackle.

The lady, looking flushed, said she was sorry but Jack wasn't what she had in mind. No, no, no, I said, Jack is just choosing this moment to be *passive*-aggressive, because he is so determined to make me look bad. Her look said, "Oh, so everything is about you." Give him a chance, I said, he gets along with women. Mainly, I think, because she felt obliged not to leave him in this abusive environment, she sighed and acquiesced. I wrangled him into a cardboard box to load into her backseat. As I was about to close the door, Jack stuck his head out through a hole in the box. For the first time, he looked me squarely in the eye.

His look was hurt. Incredulous. It said, clear as day, "You didn't *like* me?"

Ollie, the horse, was likeability equinified. Though he got too old for riding, he let toddlers be placed on his back. I saw a cat on his back more than once. And at night when he entered his stall, which was built into the back of the garage, the chickens would hop onto one of his hay bales, then onto his back, then onto his head, then onto a rafter to roost. During the day he would graze in our neighbor's meadow, muse, and amble. He produced manure for the garden, which I would gather in a wheelbarrow as he looked at me and clearly wondered, "Uh . . . you realize what that is?" His only bad habit was getting through his fence and going down to the town library, whose lawn was greener.

His eyesight was going bad. I would spice up his life, and mine, by throwing apples from a distance onto the slope uphill of him. If tossed just right they would roll down and come to a stop close to his nose. He would sniff, peer around, consider, shrug, and enjoy.

I believe, then, that my inability to get onto the same page with a particular rooster is no indication that if I were writing this in a barnyard, no pig would nose my laptop. I feel obliged at this point, however, to mention that every pig has grounds for anxiety, vis-à-vis people. Let me take this opportunity to express my admiration for the dark, Dickensian *Babe: Pig in the City*, a much better movie (the orangutan should have received an Oscar nomination) than the original, more popular, *Babe*. But in both of those films, as in any honest appreciation of our friends the barnyard animals, the issue arises that many of them will, given the nature of things, end up on our friend the dinner table. I know of a place in the Florida pan-handle that claims it can convert hogs, walking around, to long-link sausages in twenty minutes. How much of this registers on a growing pig? A pig may believe as follows:

> I'm the center of the universe.
> Let's start with that.
> So why wouldn't the universe
> Want me to be fat?

I would rather believe that, myself, than something I once heard a celebrity assert on television: that it is immoral to eat anything that has a face. I don't think I could get by on vegetables and oysters. I need, now and then, to chew flesh:

> Cold, warm, or hot meat,
> Sliced thick or thin.
> I guess I've just got meat
> Under my skin.

Except under highly exceptional circumstances, I don't think chickens ever exactly make any but the most fleeting eye contact, even with each other—even with the inimitably engaging eye of Valerie Shaff. But there is no denying that a chicken has a face. And there is a case to be made that chickens, if they could look at things objectively, would be glad that they, and their eggs, taste good to people. Not for people's sake, but because that is why chickens have become so established. To assume, however, that tastiness is chickens' life would be unobjective of us.

Mass production of meat is outside the purview of this book. Once I toured a chicken-processing plant in Maryland. Although I went through it backwards, so that the process appeared to be one of assembling chickens, the sight was not pretty. *Chain chain chain, chain of food.* On humanitarian and ecological grounds, future generations may sneer at our raising of animals for protein. But those generations will not have the experience of bonding with livestock. "Who that has ever lived and loved," wrote Clarence Day, "can look upon an egg unmoved?" Who that has ever ruminated or nursed can look a cow in the face without feeling the commonality of mammals?

I don't have a barn, but I know people who do. Ellen Pearson, several of whose animals appear in these pages, says cows and horses relish leftover loaves of Italian tomato, basil, and garlic bread. The seasonings must all be exhaustively savored in the cud, because they don't show up in the milk. Nick Hardcastle says he has a big, burly barn cat that not only eats the other cats' food but pins their heads to the ground with his feet while he does so. Sheep, I am told, will clean up your garden at the end of the summer—they'll even polish off all those gargantuan residual zucchinis if you'll chop them up. Raising sheep is unprofitable these days, with artificial "fleece" supplanting wool in the clothing markets. So who will eat those zucchinis? And will people cease to understand the expression, "The grass is always greener down at the library"?

Jill Jakes, a former judge who raises sheep as a hobby, says, "They really do believe that the hay on the other side of any obstacle is better than what's on their side." Her sheep are frequently so attracted to one another's fodder that they get their heads stuck in the narrow spaces between the slats that separate their enclosures within the barn, and they won't pull back, they'll just munch placidly at whatever their trapped heads can reach until someone saws them out. When, however, the person who is their food contact exhibits behavior that is outside the box, they unite in protest. "One time I was playing music in the barn, and I started dancing—Oh! The sheep were scandalized! They all backed into the far corners. They didn't know what this might mean for their future, for their next feeding." Jill never slaughters her sheep—"Oh, I *couldn't*"—but she does shear them, which "is a traumatic event for them—they don't recognize each other afterwards. The wool around their face gives them a lot of their character. They have to get used to each other all over again."

By the way, Jill says, "Rams love to be scratched on top of the buttocks. They go into a transport of bliss. And—my dog Clothilde is crazy about certain sheep. She licks their ears. I saw her doing this, and—no, I don't lick their ears—but now I do stroke the inside of their ears gently, and I whisper into their ears. Their eyes close instantly."

What does she whisper?

"Oh, 'Such a sweet good smart fellow'—same thing I whisper to guys."

I can't see it working with a rooster.

Am I pig enough for you yet?

You may not believe this,
Because I'm a sheep,
But I am not getting
Near enough sleep.

I start to doze off . . .
My heart starts thumping.
Someone somewhere
Is counting me jumping.

Oh.
Yes. Flies,
On one's nose
And in one's eyes.
So it goes,
I suppose.
No?

Mud.

It's in my blood.

And as for slop—

Let's not talk shop.

There is nothing which is
So good for the soul
As when you've got itches,
To get down and roll.

Rooty-toot-toot, rooty-toot-toot,

We are the girls from the Institute.

No one feeds me.
Do I look annoyed?
I have to be edgy.
I'm self-employed.

I'm well geared

To stand in stud.

Not been steered.

Got that, Bud?

"Cockadoodle," he goes.

And sows.

And this is what I reap:

"Peep." "Peep." "Peep." "Peep."

I am the cat of this community—
Looking for targets of opportunity.
Let the cows graze, let the pigs wallow.
My eye right now is on a swallow.

I stand out here from dawn to dusk a-ruminating, yet
I haven't thought of anything illuminating yet.

The reason why, I think, is that instead of gains and losses,
What I'm into, bottom line, is . . . watchamacallit. Process.

This *wild* turkey came into the yard
And said, "Brother, *we're* smart.
It's you guys who're tame,
Who bring down the name."

"Listen," I said—as he flew off
And the farmer came out and blew off
His head—I said, and these were my words,
"At least *we* don't start thinking we're birds."

Shakin' bacon, work it!
All around the snout.
That's the hoky-porky
I'm talking about.

Whiffy is my muzzle,
Fluffy is my hair.
If you want a nuzzle,
I'm your little mare.

Don't give me that "finger-lickin'."
I am another kind of chicken.

I don't know, and don't care, whether
You're able to comprehend at all
The sort of breeding it takes to feather
A head like mine. Just, will you, call
Someone to get my things together?
I'm due at the Agricultural Ball.

A little more variety, and this would be sublime.

So much timothy, and so little thyme.

We do not "moo."
It's more like *oooom*.
We can't control who
Does what to whom
But—you're consumers?
We are *oooom*-ers.

They come down here from Washington
And say they have to "pasteurize"
Our milk. Why don't they find someone
To drink it who is pasture-wise?

"How's tricks, Duck?"

"Not bad, Cat."

"Not that I care."

"I hear that."

No, I'm not a jackass,
Thank you, I'm a jenny.
Yes, I hee-haw. Yes.
What do you want, a whinny?

In Texas, Ohio, Massachusetts,

Here's what is for certain:

If you cross paths with an angry goose, it's

Your butt will be hurtin'.

Would I rather be a house cat? Please.

Not at any price.

I've got so many tight places to squeeze

Into. And oh, my God, the mice!

Getting together like this is nice.

For who will cuddle a mouse, but mice?

"Hey, Billy the Kid," they go to me.

"When are you ever gonna grow a goatee?"

I don't have horns to butt with yet,

But none of those guys had better get

My goat when I do get the goat thing going,

Because if they do, I'll go . . . *boing*.

My politics are simple: I feel
Strongly about one issue: veal.

My legs are still a little wobbly,
But I'll grow strong as mama, prob'ly.

Am I pig

Enough for you yet?

The more I gorge,

The more gorgeous I'll get.

Our mama done told us
When we were in fluff-down,
"You're all over gold dust
 But get the right stuff down:

"With me as your model,
Learn how to waddle,
Catch June bugs, and quack.
You may think it sucks
But you're bound to be ducks
And there's no turning back."

Peep

I guess you can tell . . .

Peep

. . . I'm out of my shell.

Peep

So. Well . . .

Gee.

What can the world be expecting of me?

We're a yard full of chickens, feet on the ground,
Being ourselves, just chickin' around.
Chickens to the hilt, not anything but,
Scratching in the dirt and making our nut.

Lemme hear it, girls!

Yard full of chickens! Feet on the ground!
Being ourselves! Just chickin' on down!

These are big pumpkins.
I'm a little pig.
Getting big for bumpkins—
That's my gig.

Why does the goose cross the road, you inquire?

For purposes which, than a chicken's, are higher.

Here I am, myself, revealed
To be outstanding in my field.

You know how it is among sheep—
Judged by the company you keep.
And yes, they're black sheep, yes, we're white.
But what it comes down to is, we're tight.

If the porcine mind
        Is not in the trough,
        It's not far off.
When pigs unwind,

Here and there an oink
        Bears repeating, and once
        In a while someone grunts,
"That's exactly my poink."

We're not here for conversation.
        Swine
        Dine.
Takes concentration.

"Moo"?

Excuse me?

I'm out here doing

What I'm meant to do:

Chew.

And someone moos me?

And repeating:

"Moo."

I'm *eating*.

Do I go "Blah-blah-blah"

To you?

Okay, okay, my fat hens,

They lay eggs

For gentlemen

Farmers (or freaks—

Goony legs,

Rubbery beaks)

Who come to call,

"Here, chick-chick-chick,"

And toss us feed.

Okay by me. I got all

The chick-chick-chick

Here I need.

Looking for me? "Ahem," you say?
I got in among your hens last night
Along about three A.M., you say,
Which was wrong? You may be right.

I go by my own orthodoxy:
Be quick, strong, gone: be foxy.

"What are you," people ask, "a lamb?"
As if I'm a curious sight.
A pygmy goat is what I am,
And I look exactly right.

Don't make a face,

Lady, I'm hip

To having a trace of drool on my lip.

And I've got wool

Over my eyes,

But don't you pull

This "I am wise

And you are dumb."

I know not whence

You're coming from,

But I'm not tense,

I'm not anxious,

And I don't owe you

Any thank-yous.

Nice to know you.

You will never know, fully,

What it means to be woolly.

I am

The wham

Bam

Thank you ma'am

Ram

What am.

If people knew

    I know

        How humans sound

When we hear them talk about "horsing around."

I feel like giving them a nip and confiding

How little they know

    I know

        about horseback riding.

Sitting up there, flicking that crop.

How'd they like to try it with me—

        Oh, stop!

So he goes, "Goodness' sake,
　　You're so . . .
　　Snowy, downy, pure." So
I'm like, "Oh, Drake."

My life is not complex.
I eat grass, I have sex.

I ruminate
On what I ate—
Chew it over.
Especially, clover.

I low.
I go
With the flow.

I give birth.
I'm okay with my girth.

Every once in a while,
One of the girls will bellow,
But life on the whole
Among cows is mellow.
Here a moo from Cindy Lou,
There, from June, a poot.
Mary Alice makes a moue.
All the rest is moot.

So you're a person—*someone*, perforce.

Well, even among horses, I am a horse.

To get to be my size
You got to prioritize:

A.   Eat.

B.   Be.

Z.   Fret.

I haven't got beyond B, yet.

None of your whys, wherefores, or whithers—
This little canter comes straight from my withers.

Flowers smell all the more
Interesting to a herbivore.

We're llamas,

We're mamas,

We're trotters and standees.

We're grazing

And gazing . . .

Where are the Andes?

Trees freeze,
Except for leaves the breeze
Is strumming.
Back roads wander.

Nothing hangs loose
Like a long-neck goose
Who believes she sees
Her gander coming.

You may look in my eyes,
Call me "wise,"
Imagine what flight's like,
What seeing at night's like.

Will you know
What I do, though?
Or what you don't?
No, you won't.